Using Resources to Build

by Jennifer Boudart

Table of Contents

D1708457

I need to know these words.

boards

house

logs

lumber

sand

stone

What Resources Do Builders Use?

Look at this house. The builders used wood. The wood is a resource. The builders used stone. The stone is a resource, too.

▲ The wood makes the house strong. The stone makes the house strong.

Look inside the house. The builders used wood for the stairs. The builders used stone for the floor.

stone

wood

▲ This house is strong.

The wood and the stone come from nature. The wood and the stone are natural resources. All natural resources come from nature.

▲ What natural resources do you see?

Many houses have windows. The windows are glass. People use sand to make glass. The sand comes from stone. The stone comes from nature.

▲ The glass is clear.

How Do Logs Become Lumber?

This truck carries logs. The logs come from trees. The builders do not use the logs yet.

▲ A truck carries logs to a sawmill.

First the logs go to a sawmill.
The workers cut the logs into flat boards.
The boards are different sizes.

▲ These boards were logs.

Next the workers dry the boards.
The boards dry in an oven.
Then the boards are stronger.

oven

▲ A fire in this big oven dries the boards.

Now the boards are lumber. The builders can buy the lumber at a store.

▲ A builder uses many types of lumber.

Where Do Builders Get Stone?

Some stone is under the ground.
The workers dig up the stone.
The builders do not use the stone yet.

▲ This worker digs to find stone.

First the stone must go through
a crusher. A crusher breaks
the stone into pieces.

▲ The crusher breaks the stone into small pieces.

Next the workers load the pieces onto many trucks. The pieces go to many factories.

▲ This truck takes the stone to a factory.

The factories make tiles from the stone. Then the builders use the tiles in houses.

▲ This worker makes a floor with these tiles.

People use wood to build houses.
Have you seen a house made of wood?
People use stone to build, too. Have
you seen a house made of stone?